2

D1307659

CONEHEADS

THE LIFE AND TIMES OF BELDAR CONEHEAD

CONEHEADS

THE LIFE AND TIMES OF BELDAR CONEHEAD

*As told to Gorman Seedling,
INS Commissioner, Retired*

By Tom Davis and Dan Aykroyd

Photographs by Murray Close

Featured illustrations by John Daveikis

HYPERION

Dr. Mimi "Mrs. Davis" Raleigh: Authors' Right Hand
Jason Korfine: Special Assistant, Earth
Alex Nhancale: Special Assistant, Earth
Liz Siegel: Special Assistant, Remulak

Saturday Night Live is under license from NBC.
Coneheads under authorization from NBC and Paramount.
Coneheads is protected by trademark.

Cover and book design by Charles Kreloff
for Cader Books.

ISBN: 1-56282-764-2

First Edition
10 9 8 7 6 5 4 3 2 1

CONTENTS

INTRODUCTION

This is the record of my conversations with Beldar Conehead during the journey (of approximately two Earth weeks) from Remulak to Earth. During this time, Beldar was my Master and I was a slave with an electrode control-collar around my throat. How I came to be on an intergalactic starcruiser trading stories with a Coneheaded extraterrestrial on my way to Earth—that is another story.

Prior to this odyssey, as an officer of the Immigration and Naturalization Service, I had been obsessed by a small family of illegal aliens with huge heads. They eluded me for several years. I knew they were from outer space—we all did. But until there was an arrest and a positive ID, we were not going to announce that we had extraterrestrials violating immigration laws.

And for a moment it looked as if it was going to go my way; there they were. Three Coneheads, helplessly surrounded by my agents in their stalled car at the end of a cul-de-sac. Victory was mine—but only for a moment. Then my world changed forever.

Suddenly, a pillar of white light encircled the car and a huge magnet began pulling them up into a gaping maw in the bottom of the hovering UFO. I felt my whole life was being mocked. I would rather

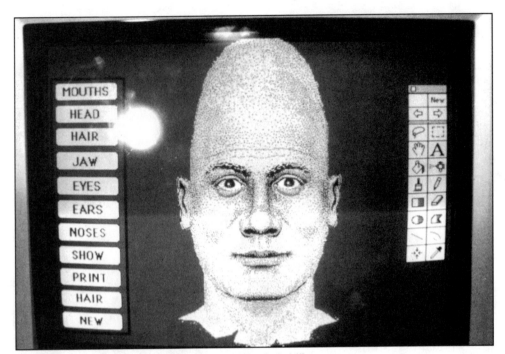

An artist's computer rendering of what we thought they looked like.

have died. Instinctively I leapt into the air and grabbed hold of the bumper of that car and let myself get pulled up into a new life . . . still, I had no idea . . .

There I was: Gorman Seedling, INS Commissioner, valedictorian of my class at Brown University, Brooks Brothers dresser, type-A control freak, stripped to my shorts then lowered into a suspended animation cylinder. My next recollection is being walked around a city like a dog on a leash. Everywhere I was stared at by an entire population of Coneheaded creatures like my three fugitives. As a slave I learned what I could about this alien planet and civilization. During our return to Earth, in the close confines of the starcruiser, I was able to query Beldar about Conehead civilization, history, culture, and physiology. The body of this work is his story, reconstructed from my notes and memory. I have tried to keep his original wording,

vernacular, and perspective as much as possible. I have juxtaposed this text with what relevant rudimentary facts and information I have observed. Where I have been less than comprehensive or scientific, I hope the difficult circumstances will afford me the reader's forgiveness. Those Remulakian words or difficult English constructions are sometimes noted in a special typeface, indicating their listing in the Glossary. The drawings, so indicated by signature, are hand drawn, at my urging,

Moments before I was quick-frozen for suspended animation en route to Remulak.

by Beldar himself, using my Bic pen on the back side of my notes, and one or two colored pencil drawings by Connie, his teenaged Conedaughter.

Conehead civilization is obviously more technologically advanced than Earth society, but emotionally and spiritually I have found them as bankrupt as we are. Their history and evolution is filled with startling parallels to ours but somehow, I have not found this comforting.

–Gorman Seedling, Comm., Ret.
U.S.D.O.J.I.N.S

THE LIFE AND TIMES OF BELDAR CONEHEAD

I AM BELDAR.

I come from a race of beings whose planet of origin is called Remulak, existing in a binary solar system in a galaxy within the Cone Nebula, some twenty-six light-years from your Earth's location in the so-called "Milky Way."

I was conceived on the summit of the highest of the three mountains on Reldelzinganth ("Relay Station 19"); an asteroid approximately 200 Earth miles in diameter, orbiting Remulak on a remote edge of its solar system in a chain of asteroids. My "parental units" or immediate progenitors operated Space Travelers Guz Chambers in a colony of about 100 Cones maintaining a Vunglerion Black Hole Navigation Beacon.

PROFILE OF BELDAR

BELDAR CLORHONE

PHYSICAL CHARACTERISTICS:
Approx. 6' 2", 190 lbs.

AGE:
22.8 zerls (57 Earth years)

PLACE OF BIRTH:
Reldelzinganth, Vunglerion Relay Station #19,
Remulakian Territory, Cone Nebula

OCCUPATION:
Remulakian Envoy of Protoid Bluntskull Planet
and Protoid Fuel Survey Underlord.
Driving Instructor & CEO,
Meepzor Precision Driving Academy.

GENETOBONDING:
Status: Affirmative

YOUNG ONES:
1—Female

INTERESTS:
Amateur turboklorzhockey,
growing Zymeg fungaloids,
Intergalactic tourism

PROFILE OF A CONEHEAD

The average male Cone life span is about 100 Earth years or 48 `zerls`; females can expect to live 125 Earth years. Their blue blood is reddish when returning to the lungs, which function underwater and in many other fluids. Their hearts have only two chambers; their livers are twice those of humans, and their retinas have twice as many cones as rods. The bottom layer of their skin is conductive membrane which kinetically builds up a charge stored up in the top of the Cone. This charge can be aimed and released from the top of the Cone, an electrical bolt accurate up to 15 feet.

My parental units', Dreldkon and Jronda, life functions are still active, but it has been several `zerls` since Prymaat, my `genetomate`, and I have visited. Our young one, Connie, knows them only from the Deep Space Communicator.

While it was a tiny, lonesome place for adults, the asteroid was a suitable environment for Conehead offspring to mature. It still brings me pleasure to recall the familiar crevasses and craters where my immature comrades and I engaged in young one fantasy activities. We would ride our viscous-boards down the long, gentle inclines of Mount Targ in the `one-sixth gravity`. I can still see, in my mind's eye, those old style breathing apparatae we wore. In some ways, they are superior to the new ones. I wish I still had mine.

Indoors, the gravity generators provided us with a "normal" environment. Most of my formative years were spent below the asteroid surface in the maze of envirochambers and tunnel-ways.

PROFILE OF CONJAAB

AGE:
7.8 zerls (14 Earth years)

PLACE OF BIRTH:
New Jersey

OCCUPATION:
Student, part-time receptionist for Meepzor Precision Driving Academy

GENETOBONDING STATUS:
Negative

YOUNG ONES:
0

INTERESTS:
Tone spewing *(special interest in Bluntskull Young One Tone Spew), High-diving on high school swim team, Interpretive Body Motion to Tone Spew with young male protogenetomates*

REMULAK:
VITAL STATISTICS

▲ Arid, expansive volcanic plains cover four-fifths of surface.

▲ Rotation is much slower than Earth, making the gravity comparable despite disparity in mass (Remulak's is ten times greater). Remulak has tremendous magnetic fields that enable it to keep its atmosphere, but there are no northern or southern hemispheres as with Earth. Similarly, they have but one weather system.

▲ Remulak is a planet with seven moons and two suns; they all revolve around a black hole in the Cone Nebula, about twelve light zerls from Earth's part of the Milky Way. A zerl (about 2.17 Earth years) is the time it takes for Remulak to complete its orbit around the black hole center of its solar system. The plant life breathes out carbon dioxide. Coneheads breathe in CO_2 and exhale O_2, as do the other animal life forms.

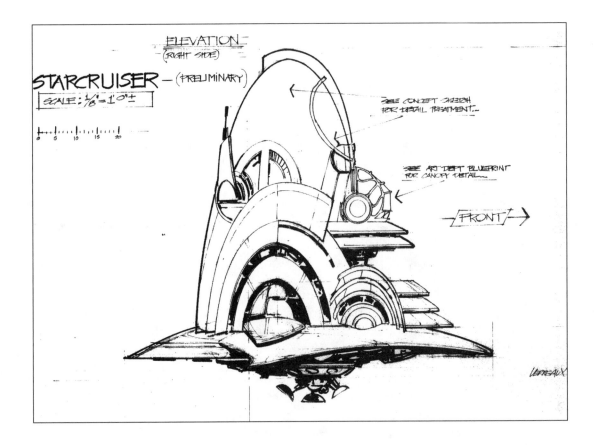

I was fortunate to be a young one during the peak of the Conehead Protoid Empire. I never knew the stress accompanied by fear of aggression or insufficient quantities of consumables. The constancy of my parental unit's benevolent oversight has provided me with a sound system of perception, cognition, and an independent sense of worth. While my male parental unit, Dreldkon, was never a waster of planets or masterbuilder of empires, to me he was the greatest Cone. He would play turboklorzhockey with me in the space behind our dwelling. Twice he took me to Remulak where we **knarfpooned** fluid-dwellers on the Sethane Sea. Because I was an "only-Cone," Jronda did not encourage me to excel in program absorption

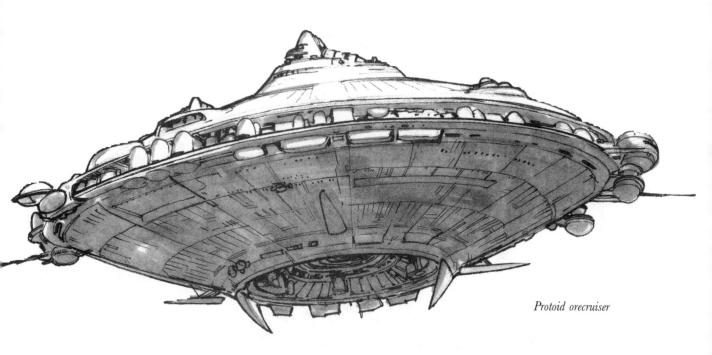

Protoid orecruiser

(so I would be more likely to spend my life on Reldelzinganth). Nonetheless, when I was very young, even by Cone standards (four zerls old), I sought employment as a starcruiser maintenance engineer's assistant or a `Reachit`.

The job of a Reachit was reserved for dwarfs or young ones because it involved mechanical maintenance in the smallest recesses of a starcruiser where full-grown Cone hands cannot go. We would strap cameras and lights to our Cones and receive instructions in headphones. Before I had a single hair on my `plarg` I had traveled to Remulak and several other planets (though I rarely was able to venture further than the spaceport in each place).

VUNGLERION DRIVE STARCRUISER

The reactors are psychically controlled by Vunglerions, and they do not actually propel the craft to velocities beyond the speed of light (not possible in this universe); but, as it approaches the "Constant," the protoid fuel in the magnochambers ignites and the Vunglerion Navigator diverts the craft into the Black Hole Universal Spaceway System. Smaller starcruisers and battlecruisers no longer need Vunglerions on board: smaller anti-matter propulsion is accomplished with irrythium batteries.

Four thousand years ago, a gene pool was separated from the rest of Cone society, and manipulated to produce a race of Mentotts with superior brain power. And so the Vunglerions appeared: a caste of mushroom-Coned priests who have a much higher than average Cone intellect and psychic abilities. Vunglerions' bodies, limbs and torsos are spindly and weak. They possess varying degrees of prescient memory, telepathy, telekinesis and those qualities that caused them to invent anti-matter reactors and Vunglerion Drive, the force that makes intergalactic travel possible.

My primary Programmer, Miss Seeranan, forced Protoid Fuel Administration to disemploy me because my programming retention rate was unacceptable. In retrojudgment, she was correct; but my immature Cone furled with displeasure. In consequence, I gained a new obsession: turboklorzhockey.

TURBOKLORZHOCKEY

Turboklorzhockey has been the most popular sport in Conehead civilization, since the days of Kuldroth. At the professional level, it is very dangerous. Fatalities and serious injury occur in almost every match (especially during playoffs). But at the neighborhood playground and "high school" levels, a much softer ball is used, as well as lower power cannon mitts, and slower `magnocycles`.

I became teammaster of my Advanced Young One Programming team, "The Brazen Nairb." We competed in the Butumious Inter-Mural League, the largest league in non-professional turboklorzhockey.

I managed to satisfy the minimal success quotient in programming retention; but because of my prowess at the sport, I received a full scholarship to the Vertexo University, where I enrolled in the Starcruiser Guidance and Protoid Management School. To earn `living-torg`, I worked in a `fast-pulp-swerl` stand near the university's beltway access point.

This job produced too limited a reward for the effort, which led me into a business endeavor with my best friend at the time, Brackster. He too was a student and we shared dwelling chambers in a converted Protoid Refueling Station near campus. He was majoring in Vegeclone Sciences.

First we collected funds from other students and interested local residents. Using this to

Laarta, Prymaat's female genetosibling.

acquire the right equipment and material, we cultivated a **gelatosphere** field on a small volcano near the Sebustopole River, north of the city, about a Remulakian day's ride on a **magnobile** (flying snowmobile-like vehicles that use irrythium batteries and magnetic fields; they can exceed 100 Earth-miles per hour, similar to turboklorzhockey **magnocycles**).

Gelatosphere is legal but, generally speaking, its Brussels Sprouts–type budules are consumed only by **tone-spewers** and disaffected younger Cones.

CONE SOCIETY AND GOVERNMENT

Everyone works for Butumious Protoid, the state-owned conglomerate whose intergalactic interests include precious metals and gases, armaments, mercenary, the resort business, protoid refinery, and the slave trade. Based in the capital of Vertexo, the High Master is the titular head who is chosen for life at random from an elite pool maintained by **Vunglerions**. The Cone Council of ten and two **Ephors** (basically the Board of Directors and two CEOs) are all answerable to the High Master and his **Mentott**. The Vunglerion priests (they are all male Cones) exercise their will through the High Master and his Mentott (Mentotts are usually Vunglerion).

Interior of Protoid Command Structure.

*Agkroth, High Minister of Consumption and
Pleasure Regulation.*

*The High Master Lerbscrab—absolute ruler of Conehead
Empire, chosen for life by the Vunglerions since IMZOORNE.
He was assassinated by a Charkusian spy 10 zerls ago.*

Plornak, Mentott to the High Master (a rare non-Vunglerion, selected from the same gene pool as the High Master).

Chysildit, Cone Battlefleet Commander, decorated for three planetary conquests during later Charkusian Wars.

Brackster and I became known to a circle of elite young Cones, the offspring of those in power. At a pleasure-gathering or **xoxoff**, a young female Cone invited me to follow her to some private chamber, with the intent of consuming my choicest gelatosphere. Because we went by underground **magnopods** and she was programming, I did not know where we were. After passing a limited access doorway, we followed a long, winding tunnel whose walls were covered with mosaics from Cone Religio-Fantasy. Somehow the significance did not register and I innocently followed my **Conestess** into a large, ornate chamber filled with the finest amenities the known Cone Universe had to offer. She produced some intoxicating consumables, both fluid and solid, then activated a pleasure **tone-spewer**. Removing most of her garments, she interpreted the rhythm of the tones with her body movements. This was an occasion that called for my best. I showed her an unusual way to absorb gelatosphere; inserting the budules into the fleshy indentation that exists imperceptibly in the top of adult Cones. Soon, nature took its course and we began to hone with the enthusiasm of youth.

We were in mid-hone on a garthok hide magneto-lounge, when the portal doors parted with a hydraulic hiss, revealing Grelnok, High Master Zoorne's Personal Mentott, accompanied by a blind High Musclecone.

The Musclecone bounded across the chamber and grasped me about the neck with his oversized appendages. He suspended me above the floor. I did not resist; otherwise, I would have been slain on the spot. No one would have questioned the death of an unauthorized Cone caught within the High Master's compound. It is **kremnarthel**. Instead I flashed a secret Vunglerion hand signal I knew from my overseer during my stint as a Starcruiser Reachit. The cloned mushroom-Coned Mentott telepathically instructed the Musclecone to put me down—causing me to land on my **sard**.

Flairndepping a frenetomate, Beldar is apprehended by a blind High Musclecone at the bidding of High Master Zorne's Mentott.

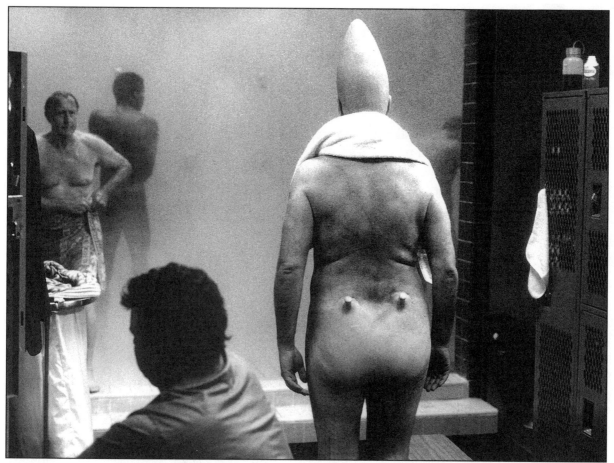

Observe the crackless sard and gorelks.

I supplicated myself before Grelnok and, in exchange for my life, pledged **Kremnoth-plail**, and agreed to be a Knarfler of the Garthok in the imminent **Moons of Meepzor Festival**. I was also assured, if I was ever again caught **flairndepping** one of the High Master's **frenetomates**, my Cone would be fed to the **grelbons** after a lengthy session on an anti-matter **slar pad** and the negative (white) vortex.

FESTIVAL OF MOONS OF MEEPZOR

Every Moons of Meepzor Festival is the greatest one, depending on who you are. In my life span, there have been significant changes in the games as they have existed since the time of Krathnore. Originally, the Festival occurred every other zerl, only when the other moons actually aligned behind Meepzor (every seventh zerl, all the moons do not line up); but now the Festival is celebrated in its entirety, regardless of the moon alignment.

Conehead symbol representing the alignment of the Moons of Meepzor.

It is possible that certain Festival Industries and Concessions have held convincing sway over the High Master and his advisers. In those days of my youth, there was no commercial side to the Festival. It was still just a primitive cultural expression. Back then, most criminals were regular Conehead citizens who, having been caught by a Vunglerion, were pitted against a real, wild garthok captured on the Sebustopole plain. Today, the increasing population and crime rate on Remulak has made it possible for Vunglerions to select criminals who are powerfully built. Some are even professional athletes. The garthok is now a hybrid whose genes are manipulated for size and ferocity. Which is not to say that the garthok I knarfled was less than formidable. It was a proud example of the wild, Great Remulakian garthok. He had a harem of twenty-six females when he was captured, wallowing in the ammonia pits of the Sebustopole delta.

MEEPZOR GARTHOK KNARFLE

On one side of the arena floor is the broad-beamed gate to the garthok lair. A stone-walled maze and monoliths provide interesting combat terrain, all enclosed by the beomothic face and arms of Kuldroth, carved from immense blocks of Remulakian sandstone.

The Knarflers are paired off by a random drawing of colored pebbles from an inverted garthok skull. Likewise, a random draw of numbered Plottsberry hulls determined each pair's order in Knarfle. Whenever an individual was seriously injured or killed, the next pair would take on the fray like a wrestling tag-team (this is no longer the case—now only individuals face the garthok). If no pair was successful, pairs would then be made of the survivors. If none of these secondary pairs were successful (this has occurred only a dozen times out of nearly 300 recorded Meepzor Festivals), the garthok was named victor and recorded on the Meepzor Rolls. It was summarily released from the arena to find its way through the city and back into the wild. Innocent citizens who are not participants in the Festival have been known to be maimed or killed by a raging garthok suddenly charging down a street.

There are no police among Coneheads. Most disputes are resolved by immediate superiors in Cone Hierarchy. But if a crime is committed or if a Vunglerion believes you have committed a crime, he's judge, jury and/or executioner. Exceptional criminals, whether athletic or not, may be deemed Knarflers. Knarfle victory brings complete vindication and, in many cases, a real chance at celebrity and power. "Knarfling" means causing the garthok to lose its footing and fall to the ground ("downing") or actually killing the creature outright.

Meepzor Festival-goers really begin the celebration the evening before, entering a Meepzor **Slar Phase** (trying to reach the **Meepzor Vortex**). In most Conehead domiciles, as the rim of Remulak's second sun peeks up above the horizon, young one Cones (a zerl or less in age), run into the slar chamber of their parental units and beat them with nairb sticks until they are roused from their slar phase. The parental units then chase the young ones (if physically able), catch them and throw them into a **gelatopool** or immerse them in some kind of fluid mass (or simply douse them with fluid), shouting "**Remdre ib Meepzor!**"

Center of the arena floor of the Ritual Theater, used for the Moons of Meepzor Festival.

WHERE INFANT CONES COME FROM

Cone progenitors tell their young ones the following story to explain where infant Cones come from:

"Magma wisps and winged-grelbons cultivate the ribbed fungaloids that appear along the rim of Moenna, Remulak's largest volcano. Little Cones sprout under the Cone-shaped laps of those spores which grow unusually large in the warm sulfurous environment. When the Cone infants become too big, they break off and roll into the crater where waiting Cone genetomates catch them with netpoles. If they aren't caught, or if no one is there, unlucky baby Cones roll over the edge and into the Magma Cauldron where they explode before actually hitting the inferno."

At this Festival, I was to be a Knarfler. On the first day of Meepzor, festival-goers met at the center of the Chamber of Religious Fantasy. This was one of those rare occasions when the chamber (with a 30,000 Cone capacity) was kreeled to the rardtips. The public interest arose from the fact that one of the knarflers, Kringold, was Remulak's greatest turboklorzhockey star. He had been caught abusing a Butumious **Pleasure Spool** by a Vunglerion Fungalo Watcher. Kringold also was spokescone for **Pulp-Swerl**—a fast consumable available almost everywhere on Remulak. I was not numbered among his admirers. (I believe his turboklorzhockey records would not have been possible without the new magnocycle.) But, as the spirit of numbers would have it, the random colored pebble draw paired me with this enigmatic sports figure.

Once inside the **Religio-Fantasy Megachamber**, I saw a mushroom-domed Vunglerion Priest addressing the 30,000-some naked Cone festival-goers (garments were relinquished on entry and numerically stored in mesh baskets by Vunglerion interns). We bowed our Cones as a second priest twirled an oxidizing fume-sphere on a string over his Cone, so that sparks and ash covered the knarflers (symbolizing strength through the test of fire—a constant theme in Cone culture). Then he ceremoniously held up a garthok whisker (supposedly from the Great Albino Garthok slain by Kuldroth on the Glairb Plain during the great Dearth of Consumable Quantities at the birth of Cone Dynasty). As the crowd chanted "**Kuldroth Meepzor Kremnott ib Icar Garthok ib Brazen Glairb**," he made tiny cuts on the tip of our bowed Cones and, with our blue-hued blood, he made geometrically spaced spots on a large white cloth triangle. This he tied about a small crystalline conolith on a Remulakian wood (rare) bier with carrying poles. Four Vunglerions picked up the ceremonial craft and followed the Priest, who led the knarflers, two by two.

CONE EV

Ten great tribes arose out of the Nomadic Warlord Coneheads that followed great herds of garthok on the expansive volcanic plains. The Conehead plainsmen used the wild beasts for food, clothing, shelter, even the bones and horns were fashioned

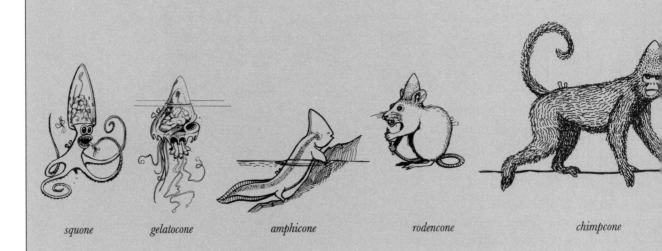

squone　　　*gelatocone*　　　*amphicone*　　　*rodencone*　　　*chimpcone*

OLUTION

into tools and weapons. As Cone populations increased, garthok numbers dwindled, and warring Conehead factions turned on each other. The technology of warfare led the way to advances in science and technology.

cavecone   *neandercone*   *nomad cone*   *cono sapien*

Our procession followed the drugged priest into the streets. The ultimate goal was the arena (only one-half an Earth mile away). There is no formal route, and as often as not, the delusional leader of the procession wanders so far off course that a timely arrival of the masses becomes impossible. At that point, two special clear-coned Watcher Priests step in and lead the procession on the most direct route to the Ritual Theater and the arena. Such was the case on this day. Our priest, his Cone saturated with gelatosphere budule foam, was moaning some Vunglerion song, drooling and watching his reflection in the gelatopool of Kremnott Square. The two Watcher Vunglerions stepped forward and put the hallucinating Holy Cone onto a magnocart and led the procession at a brisk walk toward the arena. A thousand and some Cones cheered loudly behind us.

Female Cone chorus (Krathnorettes).

As the masses seated themselves in the multi-tiered arena, we Knarflers were in the ancient chambers beneath the arena. Each of us was laid out on volcanically warmed stone tables and rubbed down by Vunglerettes. Specially brewed Meepzor `plotts` were provided in ancient `quenchorns` used by knarflers since the time of Kuldroth. Finally, greased and dressed in traditional `jalabalas` (to hold in and protect the `plarg`), we ascended the thick stone stairway to the arena floor. The crowd became agitated as we stepped to the center of the arena floor to select a traditional crescent-bladed Knarflestick from those stacked and arranged by wrinkled old Vunglerions. I was examining the hand-hewn Plottsberry wood shaft of the Knarflestick that was to be my only defense against the razor-tusked beast, when the crowd hushed to hear High Master Zoorne intone the Meepzor Prayer. Wailing from his box, he pointed to the circular opening above the Arena as the three crescent moons moved into perfect alignment.

As a chorus of nine beautiful voiced and bodied young female Cones finished a siren-like Vunglerion chant, the crowd cheered when Kringold and I emerged cautiously from the warmup bunker onto the arena floor. I remember the blue blood mixed with the sand and splattered on a glyph-carved wall.

PLOTTSBERRY WOOD KNARFLESTICK

Each Knarfler is armed with the traditional crescent bladed Knarflestick, hewn and hand-crafted from the hard-fibered Remulakian Plottsberry Plant, which is a tree-sized Remulakian pokeberry plant, its purple berries are fermented into "plotts," the potent purple fermented drink of choice. (The best vintages are ceremoniously served in "quenchorns" or flagon-like vessels fashioned from a large garthok nosehorn.)

I heard the garthok before I saw him. The beast had cleverly run across the maze and timed his entry to catch us from behind. We staved him off with some furious knarfle-sticking and managed to work our way to a maze entrance. The beast withdrew, giving us a moment to formulate a strategy.

Kringold's plan was for me to fall down or otherwise feign incapacitation on the ground. This would cause the beast to assume its attack position, on its two hindmost legs (it has six). This was to give Kringold a chance to ram home his crescent blade into its blood valve chamber. We were scrambling around a mound-like area in the maze when the garthok suddenly leapt out from behind a monolith. I was knocked cone-over-heels down to the base of the slope almost as if it was our plan. Sure enough, the raging beast rose onto its hind feet, and Kringold sprung at it from behind a boulder. His blade only grazed the thorny rib cage of the hell-spawned predator. Screaming with anger, it smote the hero Cone with one of its razor-clawed forefeet, sending his limp body flying so that it landed atop the monolith. I knew oblivion was seconds away. That was almost appealing now—providing it was swift. The garthok glared at me from the slope above; then he charged. I planted the bottom of my weighty knarflestick against the base of a large rock and turned to catch the charging beast in the mid-section. The blade shattered, but the resilient staff bent with the weight and vaulted the garthok as if shot out of a giant slingshot. The Spirit of Random Victory smiled on me again, as the hapless monster splashed into the glowing magma pit and roasted instantly in a sizzling cloud of steam. (Today the **Ring of Fire** stands in that space, another "improvement" in the restorations during the first zerl of Marlaax's Ephorship.) Two Vunglerion intern-priests pulled the charred carcass out of the magma cauldron with long forging hooks and the Conehead crowd went into primitive mass frenzy.

They whisked me to a medical chamber where a Vunglerion healer bade me drink from a jeweled quenchorn of chilled Vunglerion plotts, then he tended my wounds with healing balms, and clothed me in a Knarfle-victor's toga. Seven **Krathnorettes** led me up into the arena and seated me in the High Master's box. Next came the Flawless Cone Contest; limited to females. A rhomboid-shaped runway was assembled on the arena floor, lit ultra-violetly by protoid spotlights. The young females, finalists in a galaxywide competition, first walked around the runway wearing long dresses up over their faces (exposing only their Cones). Once they had walked and gathered at the far point of the rhomboid, they reversed

PROFILE OF PRYMAAT

PHYSICAL CHARACTERISTICS:
5' 8", 135 lbs.

AGE:
19.3 zerls (51 Earth years)

PLACE OF BIRTH:
Vertexo, Planet of Remulak

OCCUPATION:
Vice-Underlord & Envoy

GENETOBONDING STATUS:
Affirmative

YOUNG ONES:
1 female

INTERESTS:
Cultivation of alien vegetative spores & bulbs, hand/eye pigment imaging

their dresses so their Cones and faces were covered and their supple young torsos and legs were revealed, anonymously as it were, for the return walk.

One of these Flawless Cones suddenly held tremendous appeal to me—as if there were some predestined cosmic machination signaled by a physical sensation. I am not one easily given to these notions, but there was no denying this—she wore a blue dress covered with golden embroidered garthoks. But her face . . . I had to get closer . . .

Using my Knarfle Victor privilege, I excused myself from the High Master's box. I knew the Flawless Cone dressing chamber must exist in the complex beneath the arena. It was true. Every door could be opened—life should always be so. And no one could resent my intrusions while I was wearing my victor's toga. I made my way past several sets of security Musclecones until finally the last door opened into the Flawless Cone dressing room. The chamber was filled with bustling young females. I looked across the room and there she was. She was no longer wearing the blue garthok dress, but like all the others she wore a Meepzor tunic. They were feasting and plottsing as was their due, being Meepzor Flawless Cone finalists. She was eating her piece of garthok flesh as I approached and asked her to be my Meepzor Flame Dance partner. She agreed.

Gelatopool near residential structure in Vertexo.

The dance floor of the arena was covered with a flammable material. The flames do not burn if you move fast enough: if you stop, you burn. Hundreds began the dance, but Prymaat and I were soon the last couple left—the others having moved to the side to cheer us on. We ended our flame dance with a graceful salute, Prymaat on my shoulders. We dashed out of the flaming circle and into the midst of the adulating crowd. I remember Prymaat had singed off her eyebrows and, to this day, I have burn scars on my **gorelks**. Somehow we

made our way out onto the plaza. There I was. Meepzor Knarfle Victor standing with a powerful young female named Prymaat, her Cone aglow with the first rays of dawn of the second day of the best Meepzor ever.

We wandered across the plaza to the Guzzoolwahn, a hot, bubbling sulfur gelatopool. There several Cone couples were bathing as the prelude to a group **genetobonding**. The Mentott who would perform the ceremony undressed, handing his garments to a Musclecone attendant. Carefully he lowered his spindly body into the viscous pool up to his bulbous Cone. I remember looking up at the aligned crescent moons and hearing words come out of my neck hole that would forever alter my life's course. In a moment we had removed our garments and joined the other prenuptials.

The Mentott suddenly called out "**Geneto Kremeepzorglat Harg!**" And the Musclecone plucked him out of the gelatopool and carried him at a run toward the great stone Cone-shaped Protoid building, which was a thousand steps away across the plaza. This ancient stone Lyth is between two and three hundred Earth stories high and is adapted for modern Protoid command functions, and still dominates the Vertexian skyline.

We ran in a group behind them (except for one paraplegic female Cone whom I, with her genetomate-to-be, helped to carry). Rounding the stone Cone building, we dashed back into Guzzoolwahn and reimmersed quickly to warm up. We then dried ourselves and laid down on volcanically-warmed stone massage tables where several Musclecones rubbed us down with **Farthite powder** (works as a local anesthetic—very pleasant).

After drinking hot plotts, we donned the coarse garthok-wool togas and boarded a slave-drawn nuptial float. In the manner of an Earthling hayride, we were pulled about on a route through Vertexo's uncrowded side streets until we came to a Vunglerion park on its outer reaches. There, in the arid landscape, a Plottsberry Tree grew in the mouth of a cave. As we got closer, we could see steps leading down into the darkness.

We descended hundreds of steps single file, each of us clinging to the toga in front of us. When the walls of the cavern began to glow with a green iridescence, the corridor became larger and more luminous, revealing elaborate carvings and reliefs from Cone legend and history. Suddenly, it opened up into a cathedral-sized cavern. In the center stood a ten-foot crystal that remarkably resembled a Conehead skull. We gathered with the Mentott before this giant crystal Cone while he sang a Vunglerion bonding song mixed with improvised contem-

Plottsberry tree growing in the mouth of sacred genetobonding cave, outside city of Vertexo.

porary verses. Depending on the Mentott and his degree of intoxication, this invocation can go on for hours or for minutes, as in our case. Finally, he ended the song with the ritual drawing of blood from the top of his Cone, using an ancient jeweled `Charkusian knife`. Accumulating some blood onto his fingers, he rubbed it onto the exposed roots of the Plottsberry Tree protruding into the cavern ceiling. The Mentott turned and motioned for Prymaat and me to be the first couple to step up to the skull and insert our Cones into the glowing eye socket holes (males to the right, females on the left). If a Cone is not right for bonding, the socket does not pulsate and turn pink and the bonding is nullified. This occurs in about one out of a hundred couples. On extricating our Cones, the skull was throbbing pink.

The following pages contain selected images from the celluloid fantasy program "Coneheads," produced by the Bluntskull fantasy output terminal "Paramount Pictures."

Prymaat with cone.

Observance of the Earthling ritual, Halloween. Prymaat went as a tube of lipstick; I went as Abraham Lincoln, because of my height. And Connie was a medieval princess.

*Our young one's earthling male
protomate, Ronnie.*

*Flairndep! (unauthorized hone
session)*

Me in my taxi uniform, worn while ferrying humans through the grid.

VEHICLE OPERATOR'S LICENSE
NEW JERSEY TAXI and LIMOUSINE COMMISSION

CONEHEAD BELDAR SINGH

License Number

841365

EXPIRES LAST DAY OF 1985

JAN 107 N. OAK AVE., JERSEY CITY N.J. 07304
GEORGE KENNEDY, CHAIRMAN

An uncomplimentary likeness. Mebs.

Earthlings seem to be very political—every family has their own pet cause. Ours is repeal of helmet laws.

Deep space communicator.

Consuming mass quantities.

My internal combustion vehicle, with a roof portal allowing extra coneroom.

Our dwelling structure in New Jersey.

Connie in Earthling festival garb.

A happy progenitor having a moment with his young one.

Consuming a coolant after the top of my neck hole bonded with some **molten extract of hooved mammals** atop a starch disc.

When Prymaat was with cone I was discouraged from smoking packs of cigarettes.

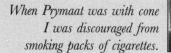

First contact with an Earth-ling—a maintenance engineer at a Travelers' Guz Chamber.

Connie in her first ballet—interpretive body movements to classical tone spew.

Connie with her Earth friends at the retail compound.

Prymaat obtaining mass quantities of my favorite consumables—blueberry Eggos, Pop Tarts, and light bulbs.

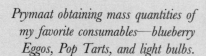

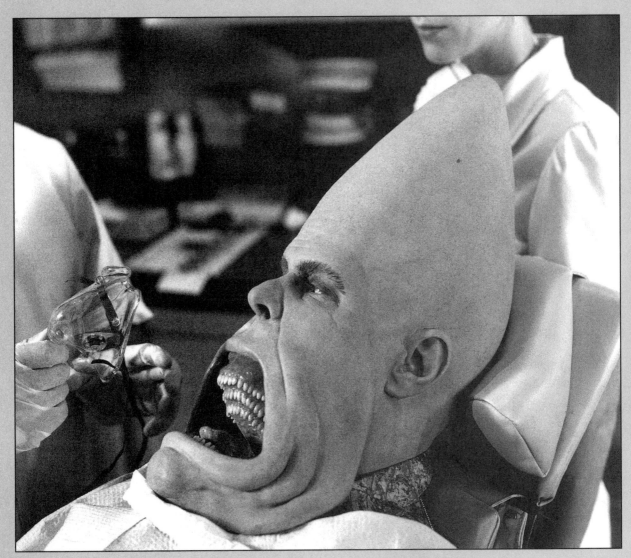

Cosmetic tooth horn adjustment process.

Out with the family unit.

*I enjoy the Earthling
sport of golf.*

A momentous event, becoming citizens of your country. "I absolutely and entirely renounce and abjure all allegiance and fidelity to any foreign prince, potentate, state or sovereignty of whom or which I have heretofore been a subject or citizen . . . ."

Later, when we reappeared on the surface, my friend, Brackster, was standing with a female who was obviously Prymaat's **genetosibling**. We were led to a nearby **House of Intake** (The Rusty Nairb) where Prymaat's progenitors and several of our innercircle-mates (those who had been informed of our spontaneous act) were seated at a flametable near the window with a view of Mount Meepzor (they must have insulated the tablelord's **nartatt** with **tidy torg**).

Prymaat's male progenitor assumed the wealth exchange and put his **torb in the flail** thus providing each member of our party with a consumo-lounger with full fare. When the flame sphere was finally extinguished and everyone had consumed their maximum quantities of **sorb chunks**, **blargg**, and **plotts**, Brackster addressed the gathering in almost these exact words:

"Greetings, genetocones and those familiar from habitual interaction . . . I was replotts-ing my quenchorn near the Kuldroth Icon in the Ritual theater when I was informed that my Meepzor Victor chambermate was being genetobonded. I knew telepathically that he had chosen the female Cone runnerup of the Flawless Cone contest because, when she lost, Beldar was vociferous in his belief that two Charkusian judges either suffered total lapses of competence or they were fulfilling some corrupt agenda. And when he saw Prymaat's genuine graciousness in spite of the outcome, he told me he had feelings of predestination. I have known Prymaat for about . . . (he looks at flamewatch on wrist) . . . twenty **trisklipps** now, I must warn her as a former co-dweller, she will have her appendages full trying to keep objects in their living chamber arranged systematically. But if I may speak momentarily with only one level of meaning: This genetobonding is not a result of gene pool calculations or of exuberant honing . . . it is an inspired life spasm with paranormal values so substantial that I believe the vital mass of their bonded Cones is greater than the sum of their individual Cones. I need some plotts. **Kremnotts** Beldar and Prymaat . . . Meepzor Narpail . . . "

HOUSE OF INTAKE

Like Earthling restaurants, House of Intake patrons are seated in chairs (consumo-lounges) at tables. Each chair has large arms from which two lengths of plastic tubing emanate, with disposable mouthpieces. The source of the tubing is serving tanks under the table. These tank levels are maintained by the waitresses who refill from large bladder type containers that pour into appropriately colored four-inch wide feed-pipes with flip-hinged tops.

SORB CHUNKS is the yellow food that is actually mined like coal, and is likewise the accumulated sediment of bygone plants and animals.

PULP SWERL is usually white and the consistency of a fibrous pudding. It is a practical conglomeration of several foodstuffs basic to the Conehead diet, most of them chemically produced and processed in large factories.

BLARGG is blue food, a granulated fungus grown artificially in large holding tanks and harvested like a cranberry bog.

GELATOSPHERE SMOKE—the budules are oxidized in broiler-type burners beneath the center of each table.

For special occasions or for a higher price, there are Flametables with a three-foot diameter sphere of flame. Each patron then has, in addition to tube food, a platter of domesticated garthok flesh (from cattle-type ranches) and a long barbecue fork with which they individually roast the flesh to taste like fondue.

The drink of choice is Plotts, a radioactive lager. A special Genetobonding Pulp Swerl (pink) was concocted for Beldar and Prymaat's wedding, with which he ritually smeared his portion on Prymaat's Cone and licked it off, cheered on by the party.

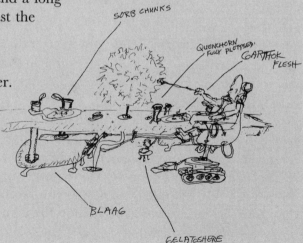

All Remulakian neogeneto-mates are given a **guzztrip** at the expense of the state. We went right from the House of Intake to a **pneumatic pod** station and took a private pod to the Fluid Craft Port of ORNKE. Again calling on my Knarfle victor privilege, I bid the use of a **turbofoil** Fluidcruiser. Reluctantly the Craftmaster honored my request and briefed the two of us on the Fluidcruiser's guidance and navigation systems.

Soon we were flying over the yellow bubbling vapor crests of the Sethane Sea, arriving at the towering yellow cliffs of the Guzz Complex (a journey of

Guzz chamber complex on Sethane Sea.

only 18 **trisklipps**). The red waters of the Sebustopole River turn orange here where it pours into the yellow depths of the Sethane. Putting our protoid turbo-engine into neutral to slow for dock approach, we saw several Cone couples leap from their cliff chamber entrances and plunge into the colorful tide.

When we had identified ourselves at the complex-programmers' control board, we were given a **fadd of plotts**, a **dopper** of garthok cheese, and two gelatosphere budules along with a key to our chambers. Prymaat observed that the key was inconveniently large and we were informed that so many Cones forget to return the keys upon exit that it is equipped with a small turbo homing rocket that can return from anyplace within the atmosphere of Remulak. The receiving nets were atop the complex, which also explained the occasional odd sound that could be heard at irregular intervals during slar phase.

Each guzz chamber is large enough to contain its own **Pleasure Spool**. Pleasure

Spooling is a parahonal experience subject to regulation by the law because abuse is common with the **honobsessed**. For Prymaat and me, it was our first time. There is an Earthling Ferris-wheel size Pleasure Spool on a small resort planet in the Butumious Chain, which supposedly can accommodate twenty-one couple spheres, the bottom half of the wheel's rotation dips below a gelatopool eight times the size of Guzzoolwahn. But in the privacy of our own chamber, we were challenged enough as we stripped and waded into the small gelatopool with the glowing, pulsing six-foot-diameter sphere circumscribed by the spool wheel. The sphere stayed in the hub and revolved by a system of magnoelectricity. The warm, soft globe appears to be covered with fur, but upon the touch you realize that it is static electro-energy. Prymaat

and I embraced the tingling orb and felt ourselves enveloped by its special gravity that allowed us to float on its surface without regard for "up" or "down." The tingling sensation became stronger, almost intoxicating, as we touched and honed. Then it rotated on its own axis while the spool turned, causing it to travel in an "orbit" which included some time in the area below the surface of the gelatopool. When we finally disengaged from the Pleasure Spool Orb we were surprised how much time had passed. Donning guzzrobes we left our chamber and found our way to the windpool.

Windpool swimmers must wear the large Styrofoam helmets and waist-strings because collisions occur, especially at the deep end. Prymaat did not enjoy the distraction of the others, especially one couple who spoke loudly and incessantly.

Interior of an individual guzz chamber in guzz chamber complex at the Sethane Sea. Neogenetomates engage a single pair-bond pleasure spool.

Garbed only in guzzrobes, we could not consume in their House of Intake. So we got a container of consumables for **remote intake**, which included fresh sulfur mollusk on half an exoskeleton. It is a fist-sized mass of living muscle tissue that is said to increase hone capacity.

Unlike most genetomates, our guzzchamber trip is not over. Most Cones' bonding is determined by their parental units, usually after lengthy deliberation and bargaining between the genepools. It is unusual to have a genetobond based on mutual attraction and after open and honest deliberating by the two principals. Prymaat is superior as a female progenitor to our young one, and she is both my soul and hone partner. Our Cones are never alone because Prymaat and I share everything, including the future.

CONEHEAD SEX & PHYSIOLOGY

With a human sense of modesty, Beldar refuses to discuss the act of "honing" between him and Prymaat. But I was able, through a series of questions, to get these images of Conehead sexuality: Male Coneheads frequently begin giving "hone advice" to male young ones even before **preplargescence** (before the child is even beginning to mature sexually). Beldar remembers when he was the Remulakian equivalent of a six-year-old, and his father telling him he must learn the secrets of honing; how to make a female reach "full-cone moan." His father made him promise to "never hone without first licking her Cone with the soft side of your tongue" (an adult Conehead tongue is nearly two feet long).

Sexual arousal for both sexes usually involves stroking or otherwise caressing the Cone: sometimes face to face Cone to Cone and/or inverted Cone to Cone, while rolling on a surface, also using the hands and body, or implements, most commonly the **Senso-Rings**.

Historically, these Cone-sexual devices were made from layers of dried garthok intestines fashioned into rings. They could be lined or adorned with soft, fluffy, or silky material of various colors and textures. The rings are sensuously placed on and off the Cone, gently twisted one way and the other, sometimes taking turns, sometimes simultaneously. When a honed Cone becomes aroused, it ripples spasmodically and flushes with rash-like color, sometimes in patterns.

There are vulgar euphemisms for the male and female genitalia: the "old fleshy Knarflestick" and "the fur-bearing squone," and inexperienced juveniles find elaborate euphemisms for the act of copulation, such as "beating the meaty mentotte in the fluid-cruiser," but most Coneheads have active honelives with their genetomates which they rarely discuss in public for the similar reasons of morality and modesty as in human culture. Monogamy and genetobonding for life is upheld both in custom and law, except for the High Master who may legally keep up to six **frenetomates** in addition to his genetomate.

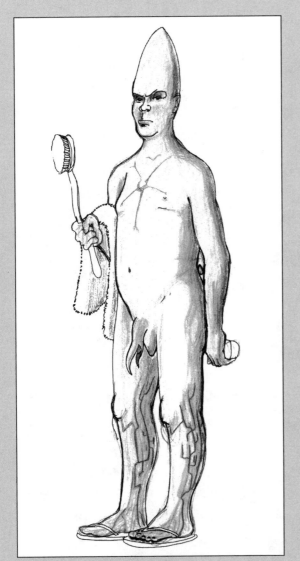
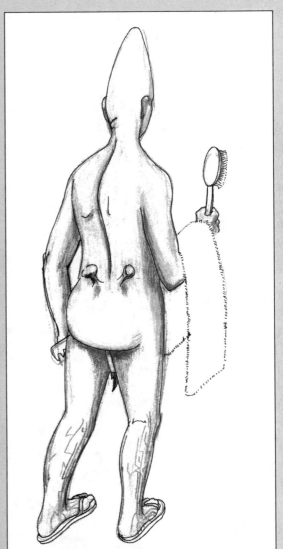

HONING AND PROCREATION

Cone arousal causes the genitals to become aroused. The female clitoris stands revealing its Cone shape. The penis becomes erect and darkens in color (being engorged with blue blood) emerging from a double-flapped foreskin, while the scrotum tightens around his single, lemon-sized testicle.

Both male and female butts are one solid piece instead of two buns (no crack), and two spotted cartilage knobules (like on a giraffe's head); these are called "gorelks"—roughly translated, it means "handles."

Female Coneheads' breasts do not have sexual sensitivity as do human females. They have no external nipples, the females' breasts must be circumcised to enable infant Cones to nourish. And interestingly, Conehead females have the labia, clitoris, and the general mouth of the vagina slanted horizontally instead of vertically. Beldar said he was startled when he saw his first bearded Earth man.

Every female Cone is born with seven eggs—four female, three male. She can select the sex to be fertilized and can selectively induce ovulation, but cannot always conceive. Female Cones do not menstruate on a "monthly" basis. Gestation is about four Earth months. Cone infancy and childhood involves an accelerated rate, so that a two-Earth-year-old Cone seems about seven. Similarly, a ten-year-old Cone will appear to be in its mid-teens both physically and emotionally. Intellectually, young Cones are above average human adult intelligence at about the age of six. But, except for the Mentotts, the average Cone does not progress much after its seventh zerl.

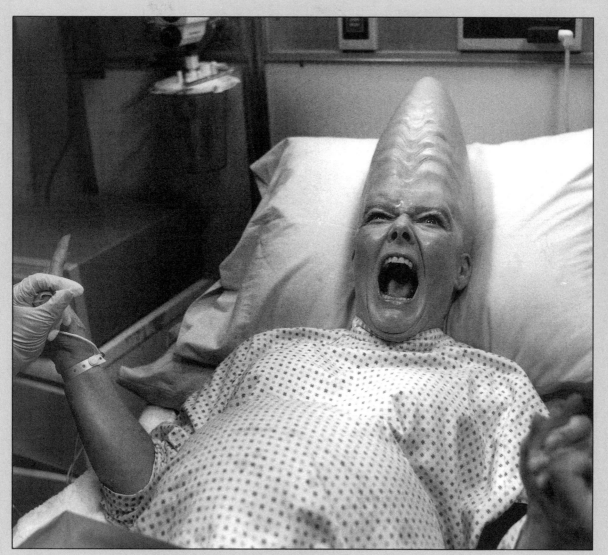

Mid-birthing spasm.

EPILOGUE

There is no ending to this "story." It isn't over yet. Some-times I wish it were. I am reminded of the quote attributed to Santayana: "Those who ignore the past are doomed to repeat it." I wonder if he was ever abducted and taken to another planet? I know if I ever see another car being pulled up into the bottom of a flying saucer, I'm not going to hang onto the bumper again. But, in a sense, I am now a man without a planet. I can't look at our offices and cities and homes, and not think about "their" offices, homes and cities . . . happening now, at this same moment. The Coneheads are different—obviously. They have big heads and they can breathe underwater and eat plastic and zap vend-ing machines; but, on second glance, they are most certainly humanoid . . . fallible, vulnerable and paranoid. As I learn more about the Coneheads, the more human they become. I find it is the differences which give me the most hope.

Gorman Seedling, Comm., Ret.
U.S.D.O.J.I.N.S.
7/23/1993

GLOSSARY

BLARGG

blue food; a granulated fungus grown artificially in large holding tanks and harvested like a cranberry bog

BORP MIP

the end

CHARKUSIAN KNIFE

large, formidable crescent-bladed knife now used mostly for ceremony, in use since the first Charkusian War

COMMUNISUME

a) socialized consumption of mass quantities
b) large dinner party

CONESTESS

hostess

DOPPER

a unit of measurement for solids; about two pounds

EPHOR

one of two such Coneheads of State, subject only to the High Master and Vunglerions

FADD (OF PLOTTS)

unit of measurement for fluids

FARTHITE POWDER

massage powder with local anesthetic effect

FLAIRNDEPPING

uninvited or indiscreet groping of Cone with intent to hone

FLARTHAG

prostitute

FRENETOMATES

concubine or mistress

GARTHOK KNARFLER

criminal who participates in a ritualized, popular national sport pitting Conehead against garthok

GARTHOK
fierce 6-legged beast that once populated Remulakian plains, now bred for knarfling in the Moons of Meepzor Festival

GELATOPOOL
warm, viscous, bubbling pools ranging from hot-tub size to small lakes

GELATOSPHERE
an intoxicating plant resembling Earth's Brussels sprouts; the budules may be smoked, eaten or passively absorbed through a body cavity

GENETO KREMEEPZORGLAT HARG
ritualistic exclamation commencing nuptial streak

GENETOBONDING
the act of getting married

GENETOMATE
husband or wife

GENETOSIBLING　　brother or sister

GORELKS　　two spotted cartilage nodules located symmetrically in the small of the back (similar to the growths on an Earthling giraffe's head)

GRELBONS　　Remulakian omniverous heron-like birds with twenty-inch wingspan that prefer carrion

GUZZ CHAMBER　　a) bedroom
b) lovemaking room

GUZZTRIP　　honeymoon

HONOBSESSED　　oversexed

HOUSE OF INTAKE　　restaurant

HYGIENIC CHAMBER bathroom

IMMEDIATE PROGENITORS

parents; *syn.* parental units
a) female progenitor—mother
b) male progenitor—father

JALABALA jockstrap

KNARFLE throw or subdue

KNARFPOONED fished with a turborod

KRATHNORETTES pretty young female attendants, who are always a part of Vunglerion rituals

KREMNARTHEL forbidden

KREMNOTTS I salute you

KREMNOTHPLAIL   salutation of high honors and respect implying a favor owed to the Vunglerions

KREMNOTTS   Hail

KULDROTH MEEPZOR KREMNOTT IB ICAR GARTHOK IB BRAZEN GLAIRB

a ceremonial Vunglerion prayer calling for strength and courage for the Knarflers

LIGHT ZERLS   2.17 light years (light year = the distance light travels in one Earth year at 186,284 miles/sec)

LIVING CHAMBER   a) apartment
b) home

LIVING-TORG   cash, spending money

MAGNOCYCLE a snowmobile-like vehicle that flies just above the ground using magnetic fields

MAGNOPODMOBILE a car-sized subway vehicle on an underground monorail system

MAINTAIN LOW TONES don't raise your voice (with me)

MEBS
a) a term expressing frustration; i.e., Oh no! Ouch! Damn it!
b) warning; i.e., Watch out; You anger me.

MEEPZOR VORTEX heavy REM phase of sleep on or around the Festival of the Moons of Meepzor

MENTOTT consultant, adviser, or Graduate of Monastery and Vunglerion Sciences

MOLTEN LACTATE EXTRACT OF HOOVED MAMMALS
hot melted cheese

MY PLUVARB HAS BROKEN
my water has broken

NARTATT
pocket

NEOGENETOMATES
newlyweds

ONE-SIXTH GRAVITY
a 60-pound object on Earth would weigh 10 pounds on Beldar's home asteroid Reldelzinganth

PLARG
male genitalia

PLEASURE TONE SPEWER
stereo system or any machine that reproduces sounds and/or music

PLEASURE SPOOL   parahonal staticelectro-gravity globe

PLOTTS   radioactive fermented drink (comparable to beer) made from berries taken from a sacred tree-like plant

PNEUMATIC POD   two-seated canister-like vehicle that travels through a pneumatic tubeway

PREHONE ACTIVITY   foreplay

PREPLARGESCENT   not yet sexually mature; prepubescent

PULP SWERL   A fibrous, pudding-like fast food consumed through a disposable mouthpiece at the end of a high pressure plastic feeding tube

REACHIT   either a child or midget who serves as a maintenance engineer's assistant on a star-cruiser or orecruiser

RELAY STATION   similar to a lighthouse in function, it maintains a beacon to aid in Vunglerion Black Hole navigation

RELIGIO-FANTASY MEGACHAMBER
big church

REMDRE IB MEEPZOR
Hooray, the Festival is starting

REMOTE INTAKE   take-out food

REPLOTTSING MY QUENCHORN
refilling my beer mug

RING OF FIRE a circle at the center of the arena floor in the Ritual Theater that burns with low-heat flames from the protoid jelly poured onto the dirt (a magma cauldron which originally stood at this point was replaced during restoration under Marlaax's first zerl of Ephorship)

SARD a) Remulakian vernacular for rear end
b) a crackless butt—unique to the Conehead race

SENSO-RINGS popular sexual devices

SCRABNORD screwed

SLAR PAD upright bed with indentations of Conehead body contours

SLAR PHASE significant term of sleep

SORB CHUNKS   yellow tofu-like foodstuffs pumped through feeding tubes

SPACE TRAVELER GUZZ CHAMBER
     motel

TIDY TORG   "pretty penny," tidy sum

TONE-SPEWER   musician

TORB IN FLAIL   finger in the hole at the bottom of a box called the consumption plect (a credit card-like system using one's finger for ID)

TRELGS   teeth, tooth horns

TRISKLIPPS   around 20 minutes

TURBOFOIL — irrythium battery and protoid fuel hydrofoil-type boat

VUNGLERION DRIVE — a protoid fuel engine that makes intergalactic travel possible, invented by Vunglerions

VUNGLERION — powerful, secretive caste of priests and statesmen with mushroom-shaped Cones cloned from an elite gene pool

XOXOFF — wild party

ZERL —
a) 2.17 Earth years
b) time of Remulak's orbit around the Black Hole (the center of its binary system)

CONEHEADS

BORP MIP

Check out Wayne's World: Extreme Close-up and It's Pat! My Life Exposed

Official Saturday Night Live Books

At Bookstores Everywhere or Call 1-800-759-0190 Monday-Friday between 9-5 EST